THE RISING COST
OF EDUCATION

BY EMILY ROSE OACHS

CONTENT CONSULTANT

John R. Thelin
Professor of Higher Education & Public Policy
University of Kentucky

Essential Library

An Imprint of Abdo Publishing | abdopublishing.com

abdopublishing.com

Published by Abdo Publishing, a division of ABDO, PO Box 398166, Minneapolis, Minnesota 55439. Copyright © 2017 by Abdo Consulting Group, Inc. International copyrights reserved in all countries. No part of this book may be reproduced in any form without written permission from the publisher. Essential Library™ is a trademark and logo of Abdo Publishing.

Printed in the United States of America, North Mankato, Minnesota
102016
012017

Cover Photo: EPA European Pressphoto Agency b.v./Alamy
Interior Photos: Kenneth Song/News-Press/ZumaPress/Newscom, 4–5; Red Line Editorial, 7, 29; Reed Saxon/AP Images, 10, 42–43; Shutterstock Images, 12, 66–67; Detroit Publishing Company/Library of Congress, 16–17; Frances Benjamin Johnston/Library of Congress, 22; Jeff Chiu/AP Images, 27; Stephen Lew/Cal Sport Media/AP Images, 30–31; Elaine Thompson/AP Images, 33; Aerial Archives/Alamy, 37; David Hills/iStockphoto, 50; Jeremy Hogan/Bloomington Herald-Times/AP Images, 54–55; Greg M. Cooper/AP Images, 65; Charles Dharapak/AP Images, 72; B. Christopher/Alamy, 78–79; David Goldman/AP Images, 85; Christine Armario/AP Images, 87; Manuel Balce Ceneta/AP Images, 89; Richard B. Levine/Newscom, 90–91; Matt Slocum/AP Images, 96; Anthony Behar/Sipa USA/AP Images, 99

Editor: Mirella Miller
Series Designer: Maggie Villaume

Publisher's Cataloging-in-Publication Data

Names: Oachs, Emily Rose, author.
Title: The rising cost of education / by Emily Rose Oachs.
Description: Minneapolis, MN : Abdo Publishing, 2017. | Series: Special reports |
        Includes bibliographical references and index.
Identifiers: LCCN 2016945217 | ISBN 9781680783971 (lib. bdg.) |
        ISBN 9781680797503 (ebook)
Subjects: LCSH: Education, Higher--Economic aspects--Juvenile literature.
Classification: DDC 378--dc23
LC record available at http://lccn.loc.gov/2016945217

CONTENTS

CHAPTER ONE

SURGING
TUITION

O n November 12, 2015, thousands of frustrated students flooded the sidewalks at colleges across the United States. Chants and signs filled the air as the students marched through their campuses. "Stop [Increasing] the Price of My Dream," one student's sign read. A New Jersey student's sign called for "More Skills, Less Bills." In Utah: "Education Shouldn't be a Debt Sentence." Students at Austin's University of Texas intoned, "Education should be free. No more debt for you and me!"[1] In Philadelphia, a drum line joined the chorus of student voices as megaphone-wielding protesters led chants of "Hey, hey! Ho, ho! Student debt has got to go!"[2] At campus after campus, the rallies all bore the same message:

Million Student Marchers hailed from community colleges, public universities, private colleges, and for-profit institutions.

the price of higher education has become too high, and something must be done.

These student activists had abandoned their classrooms to join the Million Student March, a student-led movement devoted to "uphold[ing] the notion of education as a fundamental human right."[3] From Massachusetts to Oregon, Florida to Hawaii, more than 10,000 students from approximately 100 schools nationwide joined the Million Student March's local protests. They took to the streets to protest higher education's rising prices and to help "shape the national conversation about what college costs look like today," according to Beth Huang, an organizer who helped the students plan the Million Student March.[4]

The frustrations the Million Student March protesters expressed are nothing new. Their voices are a part of an ongoing and building national conversation about the affordability of higher education. But the widespread support of the protests illustrates in clear focus the universality of the problem. It shows that the surging price of higher education does not affect one region of the country or one particular type of school.

SCHOOL TUITION AND FUNDING

	AVERAGE TUITION AND FEES (2015–2016)[5]	MAIN SOURCE OF FUNDING
COMMUNITY COLLEGES AND TECHNICAL SCHOOLS	$3,435	government
PUBLIC COLLEGES AND UNIVERSITIES	$9,410 (in-state) $23,893 (out-of-state)	government and tuition revenues
PRIVATE COLLEGES AND UNIVERSITIES	$32,405	endowments, tuition revenues, and charitable donations
FOR-PROFIT INSTITUTIONS	$15,610	tuition

College affordability is a far-reaching issue that leaves no one untouched and has effects that resonate throughout society.

THE PROBLEM TODAY

Since 1980, the topic of education costs has become more prominent as each year the price of tuition rises faster than the rate of inflation. In 1975, a student at a public university could have funded a year's tuition by working a minimum wage job six hours per week. Today, however, that reality feels far distant. More than 40 years and countless tuition increases later, an average student would need to put in at least 32 hours per week at a minimum wage job to pay only tuition and fees. College tuition is higher than ever before, and in 2015, the comprehensive

INSPIRATION FOR THE MILLION STUDENT MARCH

The Million Student March was the brainchild of Elan Axelbank and Keely Mullen, students at Northeastern University in Boston, Massachusetts. The inspiration for the movement came in 2015 from Senator Bernie Sanders, then a 2016 Democratic presidential candidate. The students saw an interview between journalist Katie Couric and Sanders. During the interview, Sanders stated, "If a million young people march on Washington [and say] to the Republican leadership, 'we know what's going on, and you better vote to deal with the student debt. You better vote to make public universities and colleges tuition free,' that's when it [action from legislators] will happen."[6]

price tag—which includes tuition, fees, room, and board—of 57 US private colleges crept past $60,000. In 2015, tuition overall was approximately three times higher than it had been in 1980, even when accounting for inflation.

Many schools, both public and private, are quick to point out that the advertised "sticker price" of tuition and fees is not what many students pay. For the most part, only high-income students who do not qualify for merit-based aid pay the full amount. The number of students paying full price varies from school to school. At some schools, none of the students pay list price. Up to half of the students pay the sticker price at some top-tier schools. Overall, approximately 77 percent of students at private schools receive some kind of "tuition discount." Their average discount is around 42 percent of the total tuition cost.

Even so, the net tuition and fees, or discounted tuition and fees, that students pay continues to increase. The amount of aid available has increased since 1990. However, for the most part, that aid increase has not kept pace with skyrocketing tuition and fees. Only at two-year institutions has the average net price decreased. In some instances,

Students on the UCLA campus protested the university's tuition increases.

financial aid and scholarships more than cover the cost of tuition and fees. Yet students at four-year public and private institutions have been hard-hit. At private schools, the average amount of student financial aid tripled between 1990 and 2015. Over that same period, net tuition increased by approximately 30 percent, from $11,400 to $14,890 (in 2015 dollars). Public schools saw an even larger leap. Between 1990 and 2015, average student aid increased by more than three times, while the net price more than doubled from $1,890 to $3,980 (in 2015 dollars).[7]

It is not only tuition and fees that put pressure on students' pocketbooks. The prices of room and board and textbooks have also increased. Room and board rates have doubled at public and private colleges since 1980. The amount students pay for textbooks has grown at a rate even faster than tuition and fees.

Perhaps the most important dollar amount in this is the one that has barely increased: the median family income. Since the 1970s, the median family income has stayed relatively flat when accounting for inflation. In 1974, families earned $62,000 per year (in 2015 dollars). In 2015, the median family income was $64,000. As a result, college tuition—even the discounted net price—eats up more of a family's income than ever before. Overall, higher education has become less affordable to all but the highest income earners—students from families with annual incomes of more than $200,000 each year.

HOW TUITION WORKS

There was a time when schools determined their tuition by looking at the rates of their competitors. However, tuition setting has become an intense numbers game. To determine tuition, a school first calculates its education cost, or the amount of money it takes to educate one individual. This number varies greatly from school to school. Some of the most elite schools may spend more than $100,000 to educate each student per year. These education costs mostly come from professors' salaries and benefits. In the last 20 years, however, the number of administrators on campus has also grown considerably, and their salaries and benefits are also calculated as education costs. Student fees are also part of this tuition-setting process. These fees pay for amenities and services that are not considered to be "educational costs." Recreation centers, transportation, technology, and sports all are among the places student fees are allocated. If any one of the variables that make up tuition and fees increases, then the cost of educating a student also rises.

The average student must budget to pay more than $1,000 per year for textbooks and supplies.

Once the education cost has been calculated, schools subtract from it the amount of revenue they earn from other sources. For public schools, this number is predominantly state funding, while private schools earn greater revenue from endowments and charitable donations. However, public schools also earn endowment money, and private schools can get money from the state. The total sum of this revenue amounts to the school's general subsidy. At wealthier private schools, it can amount to tens of thousands of dollars per student.

The difference between the education cost and general subsidy becomes the school's listed tuition. Overall, all students receive a subsidy on their education, although the size of the subsidy depends on the wealth of the school.

IS COLLEGE WORTH IT?

Across the country, many parents—approximately 95 percent, according to one 2015 survey—see education as the key to their children's success. Data supports this.

"HIGHER EDUCATION CAN'T BE A LUXURY—IT IS AN ECONOMIC IMPERATIVE THAT EVERY FAMILY IN AMERICA SHOULD BE ABLE TO AFFORD."[8]

— PRESIDENT BARACK OBAMA, STATE OF THE UNION ADDRESS, 2012

Studies show college remains a good and important investment for most students, despite the rising prices.

ECONOMIC MOBILITY

With other goods in the economy, the wealthiest people usually purchase the most expensive cars, clothes, and homes. Those with less money buy cheaper and lower-quality cars, clothes, and homes. Few question this arrangement. For the most part, the wealthy buy what they can afford, while the less well-off buy what they can afford. Yet with education, the argument is different. People are concerned about the high price of higher education because education offers an opportunity for economic mobility that few other things present. In a 2003 congressional report, Representatives John Boehner and Howard "Buck" McKeon wrote, "Education is the great equalizer in our nation. It can bridge social, economic, racial, and geographic divides like no other force. It can mean the difference between an open door and a dead end. And nowhere is this truer than in higher education."[9] Many see education as the way to provide all Americans the opportunity to live the American dream.

People who earn an associate's degree make approximately $44,800 each year. This is up to 27 percent more than those with only high school diplomas, who earn approximately $35,400 per year. College graduates, on average, earn $56,500 annually, or approximately 60 percent more than students with a high school diploma. This can translate to approximately $1 million in difference over a lifetime. Unemployment rates are also lower for those who have earned, at minimum, a bachelor's degree. Other social benefits come from college, as well. College grads are usually healthier and more engaged in their communities.

For a select group of well-off students—those whose families earn more than $200,000 per year—higher tuition rates have little impact. Their families can afford sending them to any school, regardless of price or aid offered. These are the students for whom the tuition rates are set. The point at which these students can no longer pay—or refuse to pay—is when schools know they have pushed tuition too high.

For the remainder of college students, these prices bear a huge impact on their lives. They could mean the difference between their dream school and a second or third choice, or even between college and no college.

"THE COST OF COLLEGE IS GROWING, BUT THE BENEFITS OF COLLEGE—AND, BY EXTENSION, THE COST OF NOT GOING TO COLLEGE—ARE GROWING EVEN FASTER."[10]

— THE HAMILTON PROJECT, POLICY RESEARCH GROUP

CHAPTER TWO

HISTORY OF HIGHER EDUCATION

T he tradition of higher education in the United States stretches further back than the birth of the nation. Harvard University was the first school of higher education in the United States, founded in 1636. Harvard was followed shortly thereafter by the College of William and Mary in 1693 and Yale University in 1701. Early Americans founded the first state schools, namely the University of Georgia and the University of North Carolina at Chapel Hill, in the years surrounding the ratification of the US Constitution in 1787. Establishing a

Harvard University was established a mere 16 years after the *Mayflower* landed on the shores of Massachusetts.

formal education system was important to these early colonists.

John Adams, Founding Father and second president of the United States, also firmly believed in the importance of education. He saw it as crucial for all citizens in order to achieve economic mobility. In 1786, Adams argued that the US government must strive to make higher education possible for all, stating, "The Education of a Nation, instead of being confined to a few schools & Universities, for the instruction of the few, must become the National Care and [expense], for the information of the Many."[1]

HIGHER EDUCATION IN THE 1700s AND 1800s

By the mid-1700s, higher education had become the trademark of wealth and prestige. Everyday Americans were unable to afford to send a son to college. Even if the college costs were low, many families could not spare a young man from the family business or farm. The income lost from an extra laborer would be too great.

From approximately 1820 until the end of the century, the United States saw a rapid increase in the number of higher-education institutions. This boom illustrated the interest of the growing nation's citizens in obtaining advanced formal education. In 1819, the United States was home to 49 higher-education institutions. Between 1820 and 1899, this number increased nearly 14 times, to 721. Of these, 108 were public institutions and 613 were private. Land grants from the federal government likely spurred the founding of many of these institutions.

Until this time, students in higher education were predominantly white males. Yet in 1833, changes came as Oberlin College opened its doors to both male and female students. Four years later, Mount Holyoke College was founded as the first all-female college. Many other schools followed these leads, and in the

MORRILL LAND GRANTS

In the early 1860s, Congressman Justin Smith Morrill believed it was important for the United States' higher education system to provide more programs in practical subjects, such as agriculture, alongside the liberal arts. To accomplish this, he proposed the Land-Grant College Act of 1862, which Congress passed that year. This act granted public western land to states and future states. The states then had to sell this land and use the profits to fund new or currently existing colleges. According to the act, the schools receiving the funds had to offer programs in agriculture, military training, mining, and mechanics. Nearly 70 schools benefited from this indirect government funding, including Cornell University and Iowa State University.

In 1890, Congress passed the second Morrill Act. It extended the land-grant benefits to black colleges of the South. Seventeen historically black colleges, including Mississippi's Alcorn State University, opened using this land-grant funding.

years following the Civil War, a growing number of schools became coeducational. By the end of the century, women made up approximately 36 percent of 18- to 24-year-olds enrolled in college.

The year 1837 brought the establishment of the Institute of Colored Youth, the first-ever historically black college. Other similar schools followed. These historically black colleges were founded as a way to provide higher education and vocational training to black youths, who were often not allowed into other colleges and universities. One notable exception to this was Oberlin College, which admitted African Americans starting in 1835, just two years after its founding. After the Civil War, even more of these historically black colleges opened to help train former slaves for employment. By 1900, the nation boasted approximately 34 black institutions of higher education.

During this period of immense growth, tuition prices varied greatly from school

"AT A TIME WHEN MANY SCHOOLS BARRED THEIR DOORS TO BLACK AMERICANS, THESE COLLEGES OFFERED THE BEST, AND OFTEN THE ONLY, OPPORTUNITY FOR A HIGHER EDUCATION."[2]

— PRESIDENT GEORGE H. W. BUSH, SPEAKING ON HISTORICALLY BLACK COLLEGES AND UNIVERSITIES IN 1989 to school. In the South, schools tended to be costly and exclusive. On the other hand, smaller, local colleges in New England provided increased accessibility and affordability for young men. These so-called hilltop colleges enabled men who earned modest incomes to enroll in higher education. Among these hilltop colleges are today's prestigious Amherst, Dartmouth, and Wesleyan colleges.

The increasing appeal of college during this period resulted in many more students starting to enroll in higher education, although exact figures are difficult to estimate. However, despite this increase in enrollment, overall it was rare for students to continue on to higher education. Even with the relatively modest tuition, families were still unable to part with the money or with the earnings from their child's labor.

INTO THE 1900s

As the 1900s began, the familiar framework of today's higher education started taking shape. Colleges began offering a greater variety of subjects taught, and the schools started dividing their fields into specialized departments. Universities, too, emerged from the colleges.

This new breed of institution offered liberal arts education as well as instruction in professional subjects such as theology, law, and medicine. Research also became a key focus of these new universities.

Tuition rates between 1880 and 1920 remained relatively stable. A 1910 survey of the 14 most prestigious US universities revealed tuition was often relatively low. Students enrolled in a private college on the East Coast typically paid $120 to $150 in tuition, which is approximately $3,000 in 2015 dollars. One full year's education, including housing, fees, and supplies, typically cost $350, or $8,300 in 2015 dollars.[3] This price was fairly manageable for most middle-class families in New England, who generally earned between $600 and $2,000

Students attend liberal arts school Hampton Institute in Virginia in the early 1900s.

annually, or between approximately $14,400 and $48,100 in 2015 dollars.

However, for some students, this modest tuition was still not low enough. Students in need of financial aid were given campus jobs, but often the number of jobs did not meet the student demand. Other cash-strapped high school graduates entered college only to later drop out because of money struggles. For the most part, the low price of tuition did not increase accessibility to working-class students. College students generally hailed from middle- and upper-middle-class families.

Furthermore, tuition did not cover the schools' finances. In many cases, the tuition was set at an amount far lower than what it cost most colleges to actually educate a student. In the prestigious universities, the cost of education usually fell around $175 to $200, around $4,200 to $4,800 in 2015 dollars. Therefore, this low tuition frequently was not sufficient to pay the schools' operating costs. As a result, schools offered little by way of financial aid and scholarships, struggled to build and maintain facilities, and neglected to offer key student services.

HIGHER EDUCATION COMES TO THE MASSES

An influx of new college students came between the two world wars. The percentage of US 18- to 20-year-olds in college leaped from less than 5 percent in 1917 to 15 percent in 1937. And at the start of World War II (1939–1945), enrollment in higher education was five times higher than it had been at the end of World War I (1914–1918), jumping from 250,000 to 1.3 million. At least part of this surge came from the government's efforts to expand the nation's public high school system during that same period. With an increase of high school graduates came a greater pool of qualified college applicants.

Another surge in enrollment came after the conclusion of World War II. This period

UNIVERSAL PUBLIC HIGH SCHOOLS

Prior to the early 1900s, few public high schools were readily accessible around the country. Most students attended school until they were 14 years old. Few continued on to secondary school, and only 9 percent of 18-year-olds in 1910 had earned a high school degree. Toward the end of the 1800s, more office jobs became available for educated workers. As a result, in 1910, the government started efforts to expand the nation's public high school system to reach even more citizens. This "high school movement" standardized the high school curriculum and increased the accessibility of secondary education to students around the country. By 1940, more than 50 percent of US 18-year-olds held a high school diploma.[4] Of these, approximately 52 percent were women.[5]

was known as the "golden age of higher education." In the years following the war, the government's 1944 GI Bill helped attract more than two million veterans into college, many of whom would otherwise never have considered it. In the 1949–1950 school year, 2.7 million students were enrolled in postsecondary schools. The number of overall enrollments continued rising as the years went on, reaching 3.6 million in 1960 and passing 7.9 million in 1970. Throughout this period, schools worked hard to keep tuition low to boost enrollment.

GI BILL

In 1944, Congress passed the Servicemen's Readjustment Act, or GI Bill. This bill provided World War II veterans with educational benefits, among other things. The educational benefits offered veterans "a year of education for 90 days' service, plus one month for each month of active duty, for a maximum of 48 months." The bill covered the costs of tuition, fees, textbooks, and supplies, and veterans also received a monthly stipend to pay for living expenses. Initially, few believed veterans would take advantage of the educational benefits. Some estimated 10 percent of eligible veterans, at most, would register for the program. Soon, it became clear these estimates were far too low. Nearly 90,000 veterans entered college through the GI Bill in 1945. The two million veterans who had enrolled in higher education by 1950 comprised about 16 percent of the eligible veterans.

It was also during this time that postsecondary institutions became desegregated. At the end of World War II, 17 southern states had segregated public higher education. The 1954 Supreme Court decision in *Brown v. Board of Education of Topeka, Kansas*, required that all schools abolish their segregationist policies. Although some schools had started to integrate before the decision, a battle raged among many of these schools as they resisted the court's decision. By 1968, postsecondary institutions throughout the United States had achieved a degree of racial integration and opened their doors to African Americans.

TUITION INCREASES IN 1985 AND BEYOND

In the 1970s, tuition remained relatively flat in all higher education institutions. By the end of the decade, prices had even slightly dropped. However, this trend changed in the early 1980s when tuition hikes began surpassing the rate of inflation. From 1985 to 2005, tuition at private schools grew at least three percentage points faster than inflation each year. Public school tuition increased more than four percentage points faster than inflation.

With the start of the Great Recession in 2007, the US economy slowed. Even so, from 2005 to 2015, tuition hikes were 2.4 percentage points and 3.4 percentage points higher than the rate of inflation in private and public schools, respectively.

By 2015, tuition prices were 13 times higher than they had been in 1978. They had increased four times faster than the rate of inflation. In 1980, students could enroll in college for an average tuition of $1,128 in 2015 dollars at two-year colleges, $2,320 at public schools, and $10,438 at private schools. By 2015, tuition averaged $3,435 at two-year colleges, $9,410 at public schools, and $32,405 at private schools. For many, these surging prices pushed a college education out of reach.

Tuition continued increasing during the recession even though many people were unable to afford it.

FROM THE HEADLINES

THE GREAT RECESSION

In December 2007, the Great Recession slowed the economies of the United States and other nations around the world. This global financial crisis originated in the US housing market and ended in 2009. Lenders lost huge sums of money when many home owners defaulted on their mortgages.

During the recession, unemployment levels reached 10 percent in 2009.[6] More than 3.6 million people lost their jobs. At the same time, college tuition continued to surge. Between 2007 and 2009, the price of public schools increased 10.5 percent, from $7,093 to $7,838 (in 2015 dollars). Private school tuition increased 6 percent, from $26,833 to $28,524 (in 2015 dollars).[7] Despite these financial hardships, college enrollments soared during the Great Recession. In 2007, 18.2 million students attended postsecondary institutions in the United States. By 2009, that number had jumped 11 percent, to 20.3 million.[8]

Economists have noticed this pattern in every recession since the 1960s. Although tuition continues to rise, a recession spurs enrollments. This is because there are fewer alternative options available for people who choose not to go to college, so people who would have chosen to work instead decide to enroll in

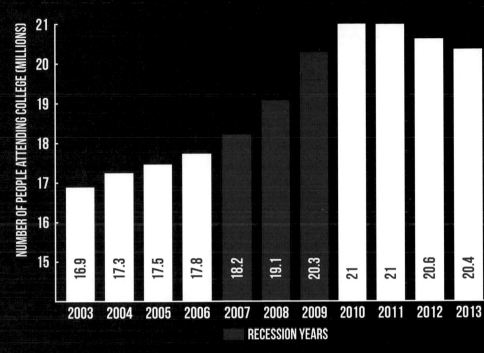

ENROLLMENT IN THE GREAT RECESSION

NUMBER OF PEOPLE ATTENDING COLLEGE (MILLIONS)

Year	Value
2003	16.9
2004	17.3
2005	17.5
2006	17.8
2007	18.2
2008	19.1
2009	20.3
2010	21
2011	21
2012	20.6
2013	20.4

■ RECESSION YEARS

college. In a recession, jobs and promotions can be hard to come by, so people decide instead to invest in their education rather than trying to enter the workforce. To students in a recession, the greater costs of college are worth it to gain important skills while waiting for the economy to recover.

CHAPTER THREE

SCHOOL
SPENDING

E ach year, as colleges release the price of the next year's tuition, a flurry of articles sweeps the Internet about the college affordability crisis. Experts, educators, politicians, parents, and students all claim to know the cause of the rapidly rising prices of a college education. They point to the schools' flagrant overspending, competition for schools among rankings, attempts to lure affluent students, steep cuts in state funding, diminished endowment returns, and even the natural rise in the cost of services. Despite all these explanations, no consensus has yet been reached for why tuition has skyrocketed since the 1980s.

Many accuse colleges and universities of spending too much money on sports programs.

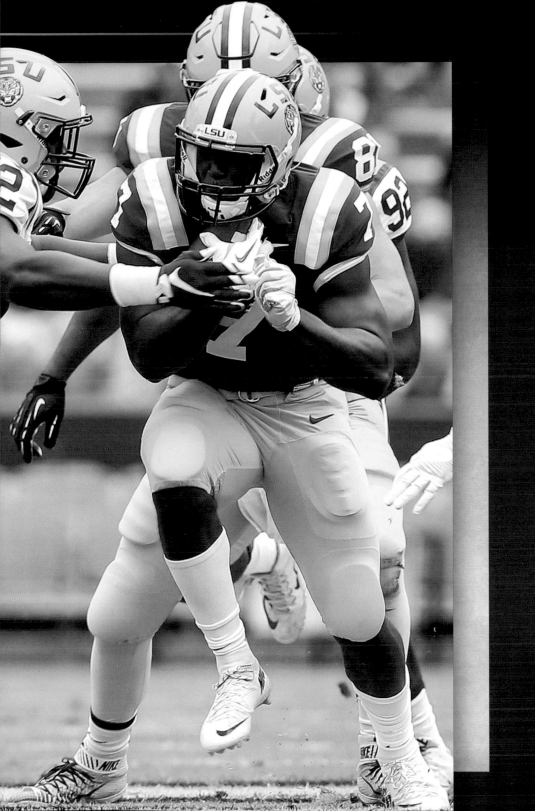

AMENITIES

A lightning rod for the debate is the luxury amenities many schools have begun providing. College campuses now boast movie theaters and spas, top technology upgrades and sushi restaurants, and posh student dorms featuring ball pits, flat-screen televisions, and private pools. The extravagance continues to the rec centers, where, at North Dakota State University, students enjoy a swirling "vortex" pool, fire pit, and sauna. Students at Louisiana State University can float down a lazy river that spells out "LSU." And at the start of each school year, Texas Tech hosts a pool party at its campus water park, which is complete with a massive lazy river, waterslide, and tanning decks.

For many, these luxury amenities are signs of schools' overspending on noneducational expenses. They see them as symptoms of an "arms race" among colleges as they attempt to attract the best and the brightest, and they claim these changes are to blame for rising college costs. Colleges argue students are more likely to remain at a school if it offers amenities similar to these, and luxury amenities make students more willing to pay the high

Colleges defend their upgrades, such as state-of-the-art fitness centers, stating students find them necessary when picking a college.

tuition prices. Even so, it can be difficult to determine to what degree students want these amenities—and want to pay for them—and whether a school's lack of these amenities would send students elsewhere.

These amenities mean different things for different schools. Some schools need to bring in well-off students who will pay full tuition. These students may not be the best academically, but they draw in important revenue for the school. To these schools, luxury amenities are a key way to lure in those students. Elizabeth Armstrong, a sociologist at the University of Michigan, explained, "If you have to rely on tuition, you need to serve the people who pay the tuition . . . which puts universities into a position of trying to meet the wants, if not exactly the needs, of the most well-heeled of their clientele."[1] For other schools, expensive amenities play a role in their quest for prestige. The fancy dorms and gourmet dining halls are a way to set schools apart from their competitors and help them attract high-achieving students.

CHIVAS REGAL EFFECT

For some schools, tuition increases are tied to the Chivas Regal effect. This economic concept describes the idea that high prices mean high quality, whereas low prices imply a defective or subpar product. This concept was shown in action in a 2006 *New York Times* article about Ursinus College, a small school in Pennsylvania. Ursinus had struggled to raise its number of annual applicants, so in 2000, the school's board of trustees voted to increase tuition. The following year, tuition climbed to $23,460, up 17 percent.[2] This placed its tuition closer to that of its competitors. That year, almost 200 more students applied than in the previous year. Other colleges, such as Rice University and Bryn Mawr College, followed suit as they too increased tuition to become more competitive.

PRESTIGE GAMES

Prestige games, too, play a hand in the college arms race. Each year, colleges and universities compete with other similar institutions to increase their standings in national rankings, such as the *US News & World Report*. Along with upgrading amenities, colleges also vie for "superstar" professors, offering salaries that may be far higher than the average professor earns. These salary increases then reduce the amount of money available for other programs—or else come from the pockets of students through tuition hikes.

Furthermore, schools spend immense sums drawing in applications. The quality of students schools enroll— and even the numbers the schools reject—all contribute to a school's standing in the rankings. To court top students, colleges send out marketing materials to potential candidates and deploy recruiters to college fairs. A study of the recruitment spending of four-year postsecondary institutions for the 2015–2016 school year revealed that public schools spent a median of $578 per student recruited on recruitment and marketing materials. Private colleges spent a median of $2,232. This amount accounted for approximately 6 and 7 percent, respectively, of first-year tuition.[3] In effect, in paying tuition, students were also paying for their own recruitment, as well as that of others who either were not accepted or chose not to attend.

> "IT'S A COMPETITIVE BUSINESS, AND INSTITUTIONS COMPETE FOR STUDENTS THE SAME WAY LEXUS AND MERCEDES COMPETE FOR CAR BUYERS."[4]
>
> — PAUL LINGENFELTER, EXECUTIVE DIRECTOR OF THE STATE HIGHER EDUCATION EXECUTIVE OFFICERS ASSOCIATION

FROM THE HEADLINES

CATERING TO OUT-OF-STATE STUDENTS

Public schools tend to charge two separate rates—one for students from the state in which the school is located, and one for students who come from a different state. The difference between these two tuition levels can mean thousands of dollars. In 2015, the average in-state tuition was $9,410, while the average out-of-state tuition was $23,890.

As public schools face decreased state funding, many are turning to out-of-state students to increase revenue. In 2016, the University of California system faced criticism for its growing number of out-of-state enrollments. The University of Alabama has had the most significant shift, with more than 60 percent of its incoming class now hailing from outside the state.[5]

However, as out-of-state enrollment rises, schools begin catering more and more to affluent students. Well-off students who may not be as academically competitive are most often the students paying the full out-of-state tuition. To draw these out-of-state dollars, schools put even more money into recruiting students.

The University of Arizona in Tucson is a prime example. Between 2004 and 2015, the school's out-of-state enrollments increased from 32 percent to approximately 39 percent.[6] At the

The University of Arizona in Tucson boasts an outdoor pool, among other amenities meant to attract out-of-state students.

same time, it ramped up its amenities. Major fast-food chains now have restaurants in the student union, and the rec center features treadmills with their own flat-screen televisions and a spa that provides massages. Upgraded amenities play a key role in Arizona's out-of-state recruitment.

ADMINISTRATIVE BLOAT

Other signs of overspending permeate campuses, such as the growing pool of administrators. Since 1976, the number of college administrators per student has doubled, from 42 administrators per 1,000 students to 84 administrators per 1,000 students.[7] Increases in payroll spending follow each new hire, as schools must then pay for salary, health care, and other benefits for the employees. At some schools, the percentage of payroll dedicated to administrators has increased, while the percentage spent on professors has decreased. Many people see this "administrative bloat" as a symptom of the amenities arms race and as a key reason for tuition hikes.

COLLEGE SCORECARD

In 2015, President Barack Obama announced the release of the College Scorecard, an online tool designed to help students research and consider schools based on their affordability and value. College Scorecard is different from college ranking sites, such as *US News & World Report*, which, President Obama lamented, "reward schools for spending more money and rejecting more students."[8] Rather, President Obama's new online tool was designed to give students reliable data that goes beyond the normal graduation rates and tuition prices listed in the rankings. With College Scorecard, students can find a school's data on how much its graduates earn, how much debt they accumulate, and whether they can pay it back.

With the increased staff comes new programs or the expansion of programs that have already been established. And with each new program comes higher costs. Some of these administrative positions fill roles that were once considered to be the job of professors. For example, today's campuses are often equipped with advising centers that offer students academic and career guidance. There was a time when professors, rather than dedicated staff members, provided these services to students. Other new jobs on campus include "sustainability directors," "credential specialists," and "vice presidents of student success."[9] According to economist Donna Desrochers, these jobs appear to improve the college experience, but "whether they represent justifiable expenses or unnecessary 'bloat' is up for debate."[10]

ATHLETICS

According to some, the overspending extends especially to sports teams. These programs have long had a reputation for being huge moneymakers for their schools. After all, the assumption goes, large universities secure television-licensing rights for their major-market sports, such as basketball and football. Ticket sales and private donations also bring in big money to the schools. All of this money, then, should be enough to cover the costs of not only the sports that brought in the money, but also those that are not as profitable, such as gymnastics and swimming.

However, only a few powerhouse public universities break even or profit from their sports teams. These Division I public schools include the University of Georgia, Louisiana State University, and Pennsylvania State University.

Despite this, hundreds of other athletics programs around the country continue to function. A 2015 report from the *Chronicle of Higher Education* found that public universities pumped 10 billion student dollars into athletic programs

PRESIDENTS' SALARIES

High salaries for high-ranking administrators—such as university presidents and athletic coaches—also draw a great deal of scrutiny. In particular, many question why student tuitions must rise while some presidents are paid in the millions of dollars each year. Often, presidents also receive other benefits, such as housing and chauffeured cars. In 2012, 36 different private schools offered their presidents more than $1 million per year. The highest-paid university president was Shirley Ann Jackson at New York's Rensselaer Polytechnic Institute. Her 2012 base salary was $945,000. But through a combination of salary, bonuses, and benefits, Jackson earned more than $7 million. John L. Lahey, president of Connecticut's Quinnipiac University, was the second-highest paid with nearly $3.8 million.

between 2010 and 2015. In 2014 alone, Georgia State University collected a total of $17.6 million in athletic fees from students. And during the 2014–2015 school year, the College of William and Mary collected $1,500 from each student to maintain its athletics programs.

Many schools insist on the importance of keeping up an intercollegiate athletics program. They claim major sports, such as football, attract more students and draw in alumni donations. Others argue that these benefits do little to offset the high cost of intercollegiate sports. In particular, large alumni donations generally come only with highly successful athletics programs.

Because they are so visible, amenities are attractive and easy targets for people searching for answers. However, many argue this cannot be the sole cause of surging tuition. Few two-year community colleges are building those infamous lazy rivers, expanding their administrative staff, or operating athletics programs. As non-selective institutions, community colleges do not fall prey to the quest for prestige as some four-year schools do. Yet community colleges have seen their prices climb at the same rate as four-year schools.

CHAPTER FOUR

DISCOUNTS, TECHNOLOGY, AND FUNDING

Although spending habits may influence the rising tuition at certain colleges and universities, they can hardly be pinpointed as the cause for tuition increases at all institutions. Recognizing this, experts have turned to other explanations that do not blame a school's inefficient use of revenue. Rather, these explanations examine the effects subsidies and external factors have on tuition prices.

TUITION DISCOUNTS

One such explanation looks at the common and long-held practice of tuition discounting. At many

In 2011, protesters tried to persuade the University of California to ask the state for increased funding to offset tuition increases.

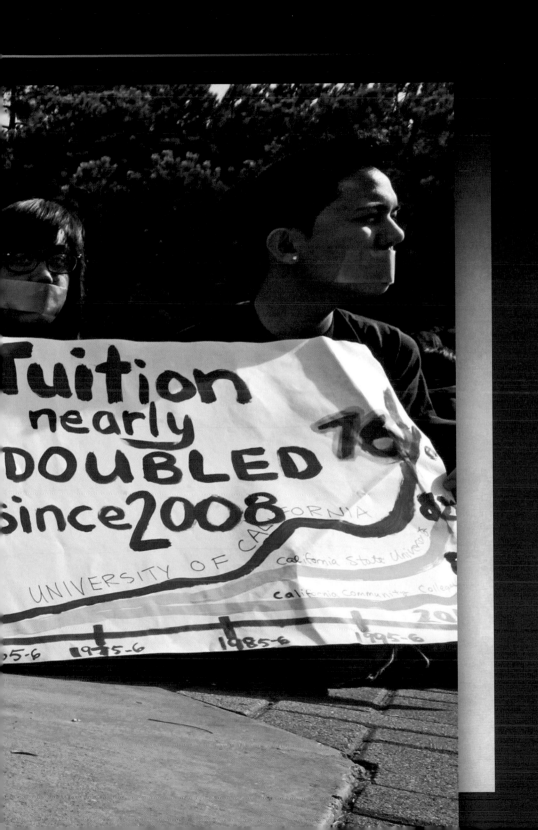

schools, the sticker price and the real price students pay can be vastly different numbers. Although the school advertises one price for tuition, it also frequently offers tuition discounts to a large percentage of students. These tuition discounts actually contribute to the rising sticker price of college. It has long been the practice to fund these discounts using the money paid by students who are charged full-price tuition. That is, students who pay the college's sticker price subsidize the educations of those who receive discounts. A 2002 study found that these tuition discounts resulted in tuition 22 to 25 percent higher than it would be if these subsidies were not used.[1]

Since the 1980s, schools have provided tuition discounts of increasing size, sometimes as a way to compete with other schools. As the tuition discounts grow, schools must find a way to bring in the money they need for these subsidies. So they raise tuition prices. The students who pay full-price tuition usually come from affluent families but do not qualify for merit-based aid. The money that comes in from these students offsets the discounts provided to the lower-income students. Upscale amenities, then, become an important way for schools to woo wealthy students who will pay full price and make tuition discounts possible.

Despite the tuition hikes, schools view tuition discounting as a valuable tool. They do not believe it would be beneficial to cut tuition and offer fewer, or no, discounts. Tuition discounting allows schools to mold their student body as they like. Colleges can offer higher tuition discounts to the more desirable candidates, giving those students a greater incentive to select their institutions. The discounts also enable schools to offer greater aid to students who truly need it.

TECHNOLOGY AND PRODUCTIVITY

An explanation growing in popularity points to the role technology plays in rising

INCOME LEVEL AND ADMISSION

When accepting students, schools work hard to practice need-blind admissions. This means they admit students without considering their financial status. However, when few spots remain, it comes time for schools to begin reviewing candidates' financial need. Georgia Nugent, the former president of Kenyon College, explained, "Approximately 90 percent of the class, we really did try to meet their full financial need. In order to do that, there was some segment of [the] class where we had to take into consideration: Do we have some students who can afford to pay?"[2] To illustrate how this decision making works, Nugent gave the example of a school with only $15,000 in aid left to offer. She said such a school would be more likely to give $5,000 in aid to three wealthier students than to give $15,000 to one needy student.

tuition. Since the 1980s, higher education has not been the only industry to see massive price increases. The costs of the services of doctors, lawyers, and dentists also have increased at a similar rate, faster than inflation. This has led many experts to believe that schools' spending habits are not at fault for the tuition hikes. Rather, experts believe, higher tuition results from the natural, inevitable rise in the cost of services over the years.

This rise occurs because higher education and other services have limited ability to increase their efficiency, whereas other industries, such as manufacturing, can use advanced technology to greatly improve productivity. For

THE HIGH COST OF UP-TO-DATE TECHNOLOGY

A key goal of a college education is to prepare students for employment after graduation. Therefore, as technology improves in various industries, these advances must also be reflected in postsecondary institutions. Colleges and universities must ensure they are equipped with the most up-to-date technology to best prepare their students to be competitive in their fields.

This latest, state-of-the-art technology does not always come cheap, especially since it may not improve a university's productivity as it would in other industries. Yet it is important that colleges and universities make this investment, even if they see no financial gains from the technology. After all, a university without computers would struggle to prepare students for jobs in communications, just as biology students would have trouble entering the workforce if they had been trained using only lab equipment available in the 1960s.

example, state-of-the-art machines help autoworkers build cars faster.

On the other hand, the teaching process has remained largely unchanged for centuries. It is difficult for educators to become more productive. Regardless of technology, a 50-minute seminar will always take up 50 minutes of a professor's time. Attempts to increase the professor's productivity draw into question the quality of the professor's work. For example, to increase the number of students a professor teaches, a school could choose to expand the size of the seminar from 10 students to 25. However, the quality of instruction decreases as more students are allowed into the classroom. Therefore, trying to increase a professor's productivity would be counterproductive.

When productivity improves, wages also increase. For example, if technology speeds steelworkers' ability to make steel, then this greater efficiency naturally leads to higher wages. In response to these wage increases in other industries, schools also increase professors' salaries to keep pace. Although professors have not become more productive, schools want to remain competitive and

THE CONTRIBUTING COSTS OF TENURE

A lesser theory for the cause of skyrocketing tuition is the institution of tenure. Faculty with tenure cannot lose their jobs. Therefore, some argue, tenured professors are becoming increasingly inefficient because their jobs are not at risk. The argument goes that some professors with tenure try shifting their roles in the university. Those professors deflect heavier teaching loads by taking on more research. Research is expensive, and when professors have lighter class loads, more faculty—and therefore a higher payroll—must also be brought on to pick up the slack. However, others point out that tenure exists only at four-year institutions, and therefore it could not explain the rising tuition at two-year colleges.

retain their faculty. But because schools have not become more productive overall, they must raise tuition faster than inflation in order to cover the salary increases.

FEDERAL FUNDING

Since 1987, some have pointed to federal funding of higher education as a contributing factor to the rising tuition prices. Somewhat counterintuitively, they claim that increases in federal funding, not decreases, enable schools to increase their tuition year after year. This idea originated with William J. Bennett, then the secretary of education in the Ronald Reagan administration. He responded to Americans' frustrations with surging tuition with an opinion piece in the *New York Times*. In it, he claimed that federal aid allowed colleges and universities to continually raise their prices, "confident that Federal loan subsidies would help cushion the increase."[3] He noted that in 1978, federal subsidies became available to many more students, and starting in 1980, the upward trend of tuition prices began.

Since then, researchers have examined Bennett's hypothesis further, to mixed results. In 2006, the economist Richard Vedder estimated one dollar in federal aid increased tuition by 35 cents, and a 2015 study from the Federal Reserve found tuition could increase by up to 65 cents for every federal student aid dollar

> "FEDERAL STUDENT AID POLICIES DO NOT CAUSE COLLEGE PRICE INFLATION, BUT THERE IS LITTLE DOUBT THAT THEY HELP MAKE IT POSSIBLE."[4]
>
> **— WILLIAM BENNETT, FORMER SECRETARY OF EDUCATION**

contributed. However, a 2001 study from the National Center for Education Statistics determined there was no correlation between federal funding and rising tuition. Many other studies have found conflicting effects of grant aid, including that federal aid increases out-of-state tuition but not in-state, more Pell Grant dollars led to lower tuition at private institutions, and more Pell Grant money resulted in raised in-state tuition. Established in 1972, Pell Grants are the centerpiece of the federal government's financial

From 1995 to 2015, college enrollment had gone up by nearly 50 percent, a pace with which state funding could not keep up.

aid. They are available for low-income students working toward an undergraduate degree. As a whole, while some believe the hypothesis that federal funding has raised tuition, others have dismissed it as an explanation.

STATE FUNDING AND THE GREAT RECESSION

Perhaps one of the most prominent explanations points out that tuition increases occur when schools lose important funding. Experts point to the decrease in state funding for public schools since the 1980s. In 1980, funding from state and local governments covered nearly 60 percent of education costs. Students covered approximately 30 percent, and support from the federal government paid the rest. After 1980, state and local funding declined. Around 1990 this funding covered 50 percent of costs. The downward trend continued through the 1990s, and by 2010 states covered just 35 percent of education costs. As state and local funding dropped, tuition bills rose. In 2010, for the first time ever, students covered approximately 50 percent of their education costs.[5] Increasingly, public schools became reliant on tuition, rather than other sources of revenue, to cover costs.

Overall, the dollar amount that states contributed to higher education increased through the 2007–2008 school year. However, enrollments also increased immensely. In 1984, total state funding was at $65.6 billion in 2015 dollars. Approximately 6.7 million students were enrolled in public colleges. In 2007, state and local funding reached $92.3 billion. Approximately 9.7 million students were enrolled.[6] Even though states provided more funding, it had to be distributed among more students.

In addition, mandatory programs, such as K–12 education, prisons, and Medicaid, have continually rising financial needs. After the Great Recession began in 2007, state budgets could not keep up with the programs' rising costs. Unlike many other programs, higher education is able to create its own revenue using tuition. Forty-eight states cut their higher education funding. Arizona cut its higher education spending in half. As a result, tuition at Arizona public universities soared 70 percent from 2008 to 2013.[7] Yet public-school enrollment continued climbing, reaching 10.9 million students in 2011. Overall, between 2001 and 2011, states cut their per-student funding by 24 percent. At the same time, public-school tuition surged 72 percent.[8]

By 2014, most states were increasing their spending on higher education. Yet they had not reached prerecession levels. On average, states' contributions to higher education were 23 percent lower than in 2008.[9]

The Great Recession had a similar effect on private schools, which rely heavily on endowments for revenue. Private schools' endowments took a hit in the struggling stock market. Alumni were also more conservative in their donations. To make up for these losses, private schools had to transfer more of the cost of education onto the backs of students by increasing tuition.

MORE TO THE
STORY

WEALTHIEST ENDOWMENTS

The United States is home to some of the wealthiest universities in the world. With an endowment worth more than $36.4 billion, Harvard University is the richest college in both the United States and the world. During 2015 alone, the endowment grew by $565 million. Approximately 80 percent of US postsecondary schools have endowments worth less than $565 million.

Overall, in 2015, a total of 812 US universities held nearly $530 billion in wealth. The 40 richest schools controlled approximately two-thirds of that wealth. These wealthy schools are able to better subsidize their students' educations. At the 20 richest schools, tuition accounts for 15 to 30 percent of their funds. Most public schools rely on tuition for 46 percent of funds, while private schools earn approximately 75 percent of income from tuition.[10]

CHAPTER FIVE

EFFECTS OF
HIGH TUITION

In 2010, the United States passed a milestone: Americans owed more on their student loans than on their credit cards. In 2015, the country broke another record: student-loan debt had surpassed $1.3 trillion. More than 40 million borrowers held this staggering amount of debt. The class of 2016 graduated with the most debt ever, with an average of more than $37,000 per person. Overall, the average amount of student debt in the country is slightly lower, at $29,000. But for some, the debt reaches into the hundreds of thousands.

This sky-high debt is perhaps the most prominent effect of higher education's rising price tag, receiving a great deal of attention from the media. However,

Student debt became second only to mortgages as the highest debt in the nation in 2010.

STUDENT DEBT WORLDWIDE

The United States charges the second-highest public-college tuition in the world, after the United Kingdom. Even so, no other country has student-loan debt that compares to the $1.3 trillion held by Americans. But that does not mean student debt is unique to the United States. The United Kingdom and Japan, which has the third-most-expensive tuition, both hold a great deal of student debt as well. With its students facing consistently rising tuition and poor job prospects, unpaid student debt in Japan has ballooned. In 2011, nearly 1.3 million students took out loans. Approximately 330,000 were unable to pay back the loans, leaving $5 billion in defaulted student debt. As of 2016, 5.5 million British adults held student loans.

many other effects result from rapidly rising tuition as well. These skyrocketing prices are also changing the way students look at college, choose their schools, and make major life decisions later.

SKIPPING SCHOOL

For some, the increasing prices mean the difference between enrolling and not enrolling in a college. Financial aid frequently covers all or most of tuition for students whose families earn in the lowest income brackets—usually $75,000 or lower for the most elite schools. But the skyrocketing prices can give students— especially low-income students who may be the first in their family to consider college—the false impression that higher education is out of reach. They mistakenly believe they will be unable to afford it. A 2008 study surveyed college-ready adults who decided not to go to college. Of those, 63 percent said the price of college was an important factor in their decision not to continue on to postsecondary school. Approximately 83 percent cited the availability of grants and financial aid as a key cause.[2]

In addition, although high school completion rates are at an all-time high, students who enter college are increasingly unable to finish. In 2006, just 59 percent of the students who enrolled in higher education graduated within six years. Often, it is students from low-income backgrounds who drop out, and financial

TYPES OF FINANCIAL AID

The federal government offers students financial aid to help them cover the costs of their education, including tuition, housing, supplies, and transportation. To become eligible, students must complete the Free Application for Federal Student Aid (FAFSA). Aid comes in the form of grants, scholarships, work-study, and loans. Grants and scholarships are gifts of money based on need or merit. Neither needs to be repaid to the government. The work-study program provides part-time jobs, often on campus, to students with financial need. Students in the program are awarded a set amount of money they can earn through their job, but they cannot exceed that amount. With federal loans, students must pay back the money with interest once they leave college.

concerns guide their decisions to abandon their studies. Even if they are near graduation, some students must halt their studies because they cannot afford to pay tuition or they need to get a full-time job to help cover the bills at home. For others, the student loans get to be too much. One student dropped out of college and was working three jobs to pay off her $70,000 in student loans. About going back to school to complete her degree, she said, "For me to finish it would mean borrowing more money. It makes me puke to think about borrowing more money."[3]

"TRADING DOWN"

In their 2003 congressional report *The College Cost Crisis*, then-representatives John Boehner and Buck McKeon highlight another problem at play with higher education prices. They note the skyrocketing costs "are

CAMPUS FOOD BANKS

Since the Great Recession, colleges around the United States have seen a boom in on-campus food banks. In 2015, more than 200 had been organized, primarily at public college campuses. Schools started the movement when they noticed students were making tough decisions, such as whether to buy their textbooks or feed themselves. Mark Ryan, from the food pantry on the University of Arizona campus, explained that with students from low-income backgrounds especially, they're "taking more of their monthly budget and putting it toward tuition instead of toward food and other areas of subsistence, [and] it's going to make it really difficult for them to get educated and sustain themselves."[4]

pricing students and families out of the college market, and forcing prospective students to 'trade down' in their postsecondary educational choices."[5] With the higher prices, students are no longer able to afford to pursue their desired education.

This idea of "trading down" was also highlighted in the 2013 American Freshman Survey. It found a great number of students were accepted to their first-choice colleges. But in the fall, nearly half had enrolled at a school that was not their top pick. Approximately 60 percent of those students attributed it to the cost of their first-choice school. The other top reasons for their choice included the financial aid offers from the schools they chose, their inability to pay for their first-choice college, and no financial-aid offer from their first-choice college. Sylvia Hurtado, who headed the Higher Education Research Institute at UCLA that was responsible for the survey, said it often comes down to the financial aid offers. Once students have been accepted and received their offers, they sit down with their parents or guardians to determine what it is they can really afford. And often it is not their top choice.

STUDENT DEBT

For many students, debt has become part of the college experience. In 2015, approximately 71 percent of college grads carried student debt, up from 45 percent in the early 1990s. Each year, students take out approximately $100 billion in loans from both federal and private lenders. For most students, loans were responsible for paying for one-third of their tuition.

However, student loans were not always synonymous with college. Only relatively recently, in 1965, did the federal government establish its first student loans. The Pell Grants followed these in 1972. In the 1980s, the majority of government aid took the form of grants that did not need to be repaid. But as tuition rose between then and the 2010s, so did the government's reliance on student loans as a form of aid. By 2013, approximately 40 percent of student financial aid came as loans.[6]

For some, the prospect of thousands of dollars of debt is daunting. But student loans are marketed as "good debt." Borrowers may owe tens of thousands of dollars, but the debt is considered "good" because it is an investment

MORE TO THE STORY

FEDERAL VERSUS PRIVATE STUDENT LOANS

Nearly three-fourths of students report carrying only federal loans. Through the Department of Education's Direct Loan program, the government offers a variety of loans, some dependent on need and some not. The government gives every student a cap on the amount he or she can borrow per year. Typically, federal loans bear low interest rates, and students do not need to begin repayment until after graduation.

Once students have borrowed the maximum in federal loans, some choose private lenders. Nearly 20 percent of student borrowers have both federal and private loans. Approximately 4 percent hold only private loans. To secure private loans, students do not need to demonstrate financial need, and the limits are more generous. Interest rates for private loans tend to be higher than for federal loans, and they may rise or fall, changing with the economy.

Private lenders can be very strict with missed payments. The federal government considers a loan to be in default if a student has not made a payment for 270 days. On the other hand, some private lenders consider loans to be in default after one missed payment.

in education. This education will presumably provide huge returns for the rest of the student's lifetime, through higher income. This is true—for those who get degrees. But for students who drop out—approximately 65 percent of community college students and up to 41 percent of students at four-year colleges—the debt becomes an even greater burden.[7]

Since the Great Recession, borrowers have had trouble finding well-paying jobs that make them able to afford to pay back their loans. This is a result of the recovering economy and lagging employment rates. In 2015, approximately 5 percent of recent graduates were unemployed. Another 45 percent were underemployed.[8]

These struggles have led to a sharp spike in the number of people defaulting on their student loans. As of 2015, approximately 7 million people, or 17 percent of borrowers, were in default on their loans.[9] For debt-ridden college dropouts, default rates are four times higher than they are for graduates. Approximately 63 percent of borrowers in default did not complete their degree.[10]

These debts have vast impacts on both borrowers and society. Some students, knowing they will need to pay off high student loans, steer away from low-paying careers. Instead, they earn degrees so they can begin careers in the more lucrative tech or finance industries. As a result, fewer students are choosing to go into public interest jobs, such as health care or social work, which pay lower salaries. Students are also reluctant to take risks. They shy away from starting small businesses, which are important for maintaining prosperity in the United States. Also, high student debt keeps borrowers from putting away money for retirement.

DEFAULT PENALTIES

When people default on their federal student loans, they suffer a host of consequences. The entire loan amount becomes due immediately, and a stack of fees is added to the loan, increasing the total amount to be paid. The government can also garnish the borrower's wages or tax refunds. This means the government can take money out of the borrower's paycheck or tax refunds until the loan has been paid off. However, borrowers are not the only ones to suffer penalties. Schools may lose their eligibility for federal aid if too many of their former students default too frequently.

Student debt also has social costs. Increasingly, studies report that adults with student-loan debt are delaying major life milestones. With thousands of dollars in debt, borrowers are returning home to live with their parents and delaying marriage, children, and home buying. In some situations, graduates are even putting off returning to school for more advanced degrees. Either they do not have the money to make these commitments, or they want to wait until they have paid off their debt to make them.

A key problem with student debt is that it decreases the effects of a college education on economic mobility. Adults who have only a high school diploma earn far less than graduates of two-year or four-year institutions. But Melinda Lewis, an associate professor in the School of Social Welfare at the University of Kansas, notes that with massive debt, the impact is not as great. "You wind up disadvantaged just as you begin," she said. "[Debt] has reduced the ability of our educational system to be a force for upward mobility, and for an equitable chance at upward mobility."[11]

> "IT IS STILL TRUE THAT YOU ARE BETTER POSITIONED IF YOU GO TO COLLEGE, BUT YOU ARE NOT AS MUCH BETTER POSITIONED IF YOU HAVE TO GO TO COLLEGE WITH DEBT."[12]
>
> —MELINDA LEWIS, ASSOCIATE PROFESSOR AT THE UNIVERSITY OF KANSAS

Graduates are moving back home instead of renting or buying their own places because they don't have enough money.

CHAPTER SIX

SCHOOL AND
GOVERNMENT
RESPONSES

In March 2015, Stanford University in California made a big announcement: the school would waive its tuition for students from families that earn less than $125,000 per year. For students whose families make less than $65,000, room and board would also be free.

Tuition waivers for low-income students are nothing new, especially among the most elite schools. Stanford already had waivers in place before this announcement, with $100,000 the cutoff for free tuition and $60,000 the cutoff for free room and board. And all of the Ivy League schools currently have tuition waivers in place

Stanford University is one of a few colleges and universities that is offering tuition waivers for certain students.

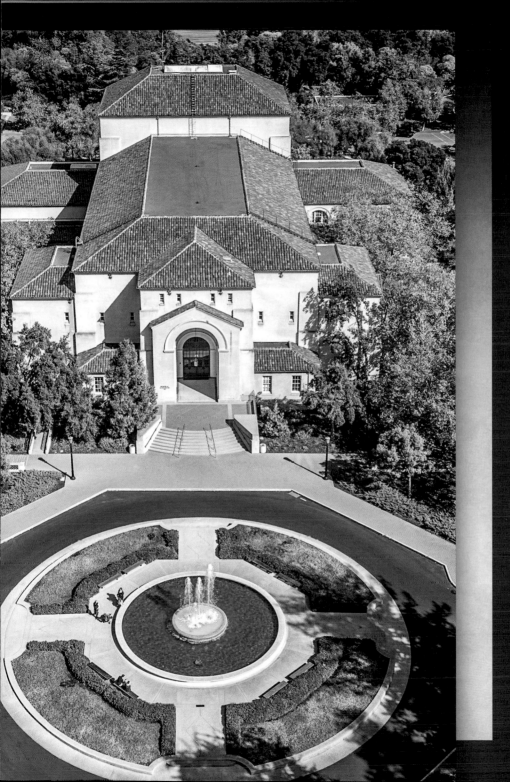

for students from families with an annual income of less than $75,000.

But Stanford's changes show a movement among schools to make their educations more affordable and accessible. In some schools, this movement specifically targets students in the middle class, who are often squeezed out and forced to take out loans to finance their education. In 2011, the University of California, Berkeley, introduced its Middle Class Access Plan (MCAP) for students from families making between $80,000 and $140,000 each year. The program caps the amount of money parents contribute to paying for all school costs—including tuition, room and board, and textbooks—at 15 percent of their annual income. In 2009, Harvard University made a similar move. For students from families earning between $65,000 and $150,000, it increased the grants available and promised tuition would not be more than 10 percent of income.

SCHOOLS TAKING CHARGE

Rather than increase financial aid, some schools are choosing to go directly after the high prices.

Pennsylvania's Rosemont College and New York's Utica College are two schools among dozens that chose to slash their sticker prices for the 2016 school year. Rosemont's and Utica's cuts are among the most extreme, with tuition falling by 43 percent and 42 percent, respectively. This dropped Rosemont's tuition from $32,620 to $18,500 and Utica's from $34,466 to $19,996.[1] In 2016, New Jersey's Seton Hall launched a program that cut tuition by two-thirds for its top early-decision applicants.

Schools also turn to tuition freezes to keep prices in check. In some cases, school leaders instate these freezes on a year-by-year basis. A tuition freeze one year may be followed by a year with increased prices. In other cases,

MIDDLE-CLASS STUDENTS SQUEEZED OUT

Millions of middle-class students are being squeezed out when trying to pay tuition. When it comes to paying for college, high-income students generally receive help from parents and do not rely on loans to cover tuition. Low-income students often receive nonloan financial aid to pay for much of their tuition. Similar to their high-income classmates, they can escape college largely debt-free. However, middle-class students often have less federal grant aid available to them because of their parents' income level. With expected family contributions rising with tuition, even relatively well-off families struggle to afford the payments expected of them. As a result, many middle-class students resort to student loans to make up the difference. A 2014 study found that students whose families earned between $40,000 and $100,000 held considerably more debt than students from families with incomes either lower or higher.

schools offer students a four-year tuition freeze. This guarantees students the price they pay throughout their college experience will not go up. Even if tuition increases during that period, students who entered college paying a lower price will continue to pay that price until they graduate.

THE GOVERNMENT'S PUSH FOR AFFORDABILITY

Since the Great Recession, the federal government has played an increasingly important role in keeping higher education affordable. As most states cut funding to higher education, the federal government picked up the slack. Before the recession, states usually spent an average of 65 percent more than the federal government each year. However, in 2010, the federal government's spending on higher education surpassed that of state governments. In 2013, federal spending reached $75.6 billion, while state spending totaled $72.7 billion.[2]

Pell Grants fueled much of the federal government's surge in higher education funding. Established in 1972, Pell Grants are the centerpiece of the federal government's financial aid. They are available for low-income students working toward an undergraduate degree. Spending on the Pell Grant program nearly doubled between 2004 and 2014, from $16.5 billion to $30.3 billion (in 2014 dollars). In 2014, the program served 8.2 million students, up from 5.3 million in 2004.[3] Throughout this time, Congress also approved increasing the maximum Pell Grant award to $5,730 for the 2014–2015 school year, up almost $1,000 from 2008.

President Obama led the way on other cost-saving measures as well. With the American Opportunity Tax Credit, some families with children in college can reduce their income taxes by $2,500. In December 2015, he finalized the Revised Pay as You Earn (REPAYE) program, which allows students with federal loans to sign up for income-based repayment plans. With REPAYE, monthly payments are capped at 10 percent of the borrower's income. The government automatically deducts the amount from each paycheck until the debt is repaid. After 20 years, the government forgives the remaining debt if it has not already been paid off. For those who work for the government or at a nonprofit, the government may forgive the loans after ten years under the Public Service Loan Forgiveness Program.

States, too, have turned to a great variety of other solutions to keep college affordable. In 2008, Missouri

President Obama addressed the media after speaking with students and their families on the impact the American Opportunity Tax Credit will have on them.

lawmakers passed regulations to allow tuition to increase at only the rate of inflation. In Illinois, public universities must give students a fixed tuition rate for their entire four years at the school. Maryland passed legislation that ties tuition hikes to increases in the median family income. This ensures tuition increases only as families can better afford it. In 2015, Washington's state legislature voted to decrease tuition at all four-year public colleges by 5 percent for the 2015–2016 school year. For the 2016–2017 school year, tuition would drop by an additional 10 to 15 percent.[4]

TUITION-FREE COMMUNITY COLLEGE

Recently, some states have started a movement to make all their community colleges tuition-free. In 2014, Tennessee lawmakers voted to create the Tennessee Promise. Through this statewide program, all recent high school graduates can attend any of the state's community or technical colleges tuition-free. Not only that, the Tennessee Promise also provides students with mentors to help them make a successful transition from high school to college. After the program's first year, enrollment at the state's two-year institutions had increased by one-fourth.

Other states have followed suit since Tennessee's success. Oregon lawmakers approved the creation of Oregon Promise in 2015. It became the second state in the country to offer free community college. In 2016, Minnesota started a scaled-down version of Oregon's and Tennessee's programs. It does not offer universal free community college, but it covers tuition costs for low-income students enrolled in certain job training programs, such as accounting and law enforcement. Kentucky legislators approved the Work Ready Kentucky Scholarship Program in 2016, which provides free community college tuition to recent high school graduates who maintain good grades. It is slated to begin in the 2017–2018 school year. By 2016, 12 other states

COMMUNITY COLLEGE DEMOGRAPHICS

Community colleges tend to serve a population of students far different from many four-year institutions. They are frequently used postsecondary options for low-income and first-generation college students. In 2012, 7.7 million community college students made up approximately 45 percent of the total number of students enrolled in higher education in the United States. Of these millions, more than one-third were first-generation college students.[5] Approximately 3.2 million, or more than one-third of total undergraduates, received need-based Pell Grants.[6] In 2014, community colleges were also home to more than half of the American Indians, African Americans, and Latinos attending postsecondary schools in the United States.

had introduced legislation that would create tuition-free community college.

President Obama also made headway on the issue from the White House. In 2015, he proposed America's College Promise to Congress. Modeled on the Tennessee Promise, this program would provide two free years of community college to hardworking, responsible students who earn good grades. The federal government would pay for the majority of each student's tuition, and state governments would cover the rest. President Obama predicted the program would affect approximately nine million people and help full-time students save approximately $3,800 per year. By 2016, 27 tuition-free community college programs had been launched around the country, although these programs were far from universal. However, to stimulate their expansion, President Obama announced the federal government would offer $100 million in America's Promise Grants. These grants were earmarked specifically for community colleges and local businesses to establish partnerships that would offer tuition-free training for students going into high-demand jobs.

THE DEMOCRATS' STANCE VERSUS THE REPUBLICANS'

Democrats and Republicans approach the issue of college affordability from different perspectives. Democrats view the issue as one that can be at least partially resolved by greater government spending. Democrats believe that by putting more government funds toward higher education, students can leave college debt-free. A few even think universal free public college is doable and the best solution for increasing accessibility, though others disagree. In the legislature, liberals have also put forward proposals that would strike all student debt, cut student-loan interest rates, and increase grant aid from the federal government.

"AS A YOUNG STUDENT IN NEVADA SAID TO ME, 'THE HARDEST THING ABOUT GOING TO COLLEGE SHOULD NOT BE PAYING FOR IT.'"[7]

— HILLARY CLINTON DURING A 2015 DEMOCRATIC PRESIDENTIAL DEBATE

On the other hand, the core ideals of Republicans are based on the idea of less government involvement and spending. Many Republicans see government funding as one of the problems driving prices up. They are more likely to support alternative solutions, such as requiring schools to pay for a percentage of their students' defaulted loans. This solution would give schools a greater incentive to keep their tuition prices at manageable levels for students who must take out student loans. For the most part, Republicans are prone to cutting funds to higher education, which many Democrats believe is a major reason for the increase in tuition prices.

FREE COLLEGE AROUND THE WORLD

A handful of countries around the world offer free postsecondary education. In 2016, presidential hopeful Senator Bernie Sanders brought some of these countries into the limelight. He proposed the United States offer free tuition for all students, citing Denmark, Finland, Iceland, Ireland, Mexico, Norway, and Sweden as some successful examples of this practice. To make free higher education possible, taxpayers play a key role in these countries. Especially in Denmark, Finland, Norway, and Sweden, governments collect high income taxes from citizens and infuse universities with this revenue. However, most of these countries (except Finland) enroll a smaller percentage of citizens between the ages of 18 and 24 than does the United States.

CHAPTER SEVEN

THE FOR-PROFIT
PROBLEM

T he 1990s saw for-profit, or commercial, colleges explode onto the higher-education scene. Many people lauded these for-profits as the education of the future. The schools appeared to be good alternatives to crowded and underfunded community colleges. They most often catered to nontraditional students, those who were older or wanted to take classes while working full time. Associate's degrees and certificates were the most common credentials awarded, although some for-profits also offered bachelor's degrees and even doctorates. Classes were scheduled at convenient times and locations. And as the Internet grew, so did the online class offerings of many for-profit colleges.

The University of Phoenix was the largest for-profit institution in the United States in early 2015.

These for-profit colleges soon became the fastest-growing type of higher education in the country. At the close of the 1980s, approximately 200,000 students were enrolled in for-profit colleges. That number leaped to two million by 2012. Approximately 10 percent of students receiving postsecondary training attended for-profit colleges.[1]

Unlike nonprofit schools, for-profits are privately owned businesses that are controlled by investors and stockholders and operate with profit in mind. Rather than receiving state funding directly or endowment earnings, for-profit colleges mostly rely on tuition for revenue. To many students, the appeal of for-profit colleges lies in their short, job-oriented programs and flexible scheduling.

FOR-PROFIT TUITION

Commercial colleges were once seen as affordable alternatives to public schools. However, tuition at these institutions tends to be much higher than at comparable two-year nonprofits. The average tuition at a for-profit college in 2015 was $15,610, while the average at a two-year public school was $3,345. Even in-state tuition at a four-year public school was cheaper than a commercial school, at $9,410. Tuition at for-profits has also increased at a rate similar to that of other colleges, jumping 3 percent from 2014 to 2015.

Up to 90 percent of most schools' revenue comes from federal financial aid, usually in the form of Pell Grants and loans.[2] To get these federal dollars, some for-profit institutions target low-income adults who qualify for this aid. They also market directly to military veterans who have GI Bill benefits. Because the loans come from the government, these schools can increase tuition higher than it needs to be, allowing them to net a greater amount of federal money. These schools do not loan money themselves, so until 2015 they did not have to worry about whether students would pay back the loans. Therefore, when enrolling new students,

ACCOUNTABILITY TO THE FEDERAL GOVERNMENT

As of 2015, the government has made for-profit schools accountable for how many of their students default on loans. For-profit schools must prove the average loan payments of its students and graduates are less than 8 percent of their income. If a school cannot prove this for four consecutive years, then it becomes ineligible to receive federal loans. Because schools are so dependent on this federal money, losing that support could mean a school must close.

schools encouraged them to borrow the maximum amount possible.

Students then fell into debt trying to pay off the excessive tuition. In 2015, approximately 96 percent of students at for-profits took out student loans, which averaged approximately $40,000.[3] At nonprofit institutions, approximately 70 percent bear student loans, which average around $29,000.[4]

For-profit schools also have lower graduation rates than both two-year and four-year nonprofit schools. In 2008, 22 percent of students at for-profit colleges graduated. Approximately 55 percent graduated from public nonprofits, while 65 percent graduated from nonprofit private universities. This has left many students saddled with debt and no certificate or degree to show for it. They must then try paying off their thousands of dollars in debt without having any better credentials than before.

Graduates of for-profit schools are more likely to be unemployed than graduates of two-year community colleges. And even those graduates who do find work are still paid less than those with similar degrees from nonprofit two-year colleges. In 2014, data from the

Department of Education suggested 72 percent of graduates from commercial schools earn even less than high school dropouts.[5] A 2015 study found employers tend to be biased against degrees from for-profit institutions, which could contribute to these higher unemployment rates and lower income levels.

As a result, for-profit students overwhelmingly default on their student loans. In 2012, students at commercial schools made up 10 percent of enrollees in higher education. They carried approximately 31 percent of the nation's student debt. But they accounted for 39 percent of all student-loan defaults.[6] Students at for-profit colleges are three times more likely to default on their loans than

THE FATE OF THE UNIVERSITY OF PHOENIX

Established in 1976, the University of Phoenix is the largest for-profit institution in the country. By 2012, it had blossomed into a network of 227 campuses and boasted a digital campus with its University of Phoenix online. However, in 2015, the government began investigating the school for claims of misleading marketing. Later that year, the government temporarily banned representatives of the school from military bases after they allegedly held unauthorized recruitment events. The Department of Defense also announced no military members would receive tuition assistance if they enrolled in the University of Phoenix. By the end of 2015, more than 50,000 students had left the University of Phoenix, and the school's stock value had plummeted by 75 percent.

students at four-year nonprofit schools and 3.5 times more likely than students at community colleges.

THE CASE OF CORINTHIAN COLLEGES INC.

Not all for-profits are failing to provide students with quality education. Many for-profit institutions are, according to Ali Wong of the *Atlantic,* "expanding access and providing worthy outcomes" for students.[7] For-profit schools are notable for how many older, minority, and disadvantaged students they serve—populations that often are not represented in nonprofit institutions, especially four-year schools. They are giving students opportunities they otherwise may not have been able to get, and helping them start new careers. Some schools are even making strides toward changing the face of education as they experiment with new digital teaching platforms.

However, there are some schools that are recognized as predatory institutions that chase after federal dollars. Among the most prominent for-profit schools accused of this is Corinthian Colleges Inc., the company in charge of Everest and Heald colleges. Not only is Corinthian charged with predatory lending practices; it is also accused of misleading potential students in its marketing. Corinthian officials made deceptive, overblown promises about what a degree from a Corinthian school could do for students. They exaggerated the schools' job-placement rates and salaries for graduates. In one notable instance, an official informed a potential student that barbers could make $250,000 each year.

The US government began an investigation into the claims. In 2014, it filed a lawsuit against the school for false advertising and predatory lending. In early 2015, the

Nearly a year after Gregory Satterfield graduated from Everest, he still could not find a job that would pay him more than $8.50 an hour.

college paid $480 million to the federal government to partially pay off private student loans.

In February 2015, a group of students, named the "Corinthian 15," began protesting the debt they had accumulated as students at Corinthian's Everest College. They announced a "debt strike," the first ever in the United States. "We paid dearly for degrees that have led to unemployment or to jobs that don't pay a living wage. We can't and won't pay any longer," they wrote in an open letter to the US Department of Education.[8]

Eventually, Corinthian Colleges Inc. filed for bankruptcy. It shuttered its operations in April 2015. Other for-profit schools have come under increased scrutiny for similar offenses. As a result, many of these schools are suffering decreased enrollments.

"FOR TOO MANY STUDENTS, CORINTHIAN HAS TURNED THE AMERICAN DREAM OF HIGHER EDUCATION INTO AN ONGOING NIGHTMARE OF DEBT AND DESPAIR."[9]

— RICHARD CORDRAY, DIRECTOR OF THE CONSUMER FINANCIAL PROTECTION BUREAU

Everest College students wait outside the school in April 2015. They hope to receive their transcripts and transfer their credits.

FROM THE
HEADLINES

ROLLING JUBILEE BUYS PRIVATE STUDENT DEBT

In 2014, Rolling Jubilee, a project run by Strike Debt, which is dedicated to eliminating debt, bought up approximately $3.8 million in private student debt. The debt belonged to more than 2,700 students who had attended Corinthian's Everest College. According to the project, it chose debts associated with Corinthian College to "focus public attention on the grim consequences of allowing higher education to be used as a vehicle for private profit."[10]

To buy the debt, Rolling Jubilee started a crowd funding campaign to collect donations. Throughout 2014, the project put the money toward buying back debt from debt collectors. These debts cost the group pennies on the dollar, and Rolling Jubilee spent more than $100,000 of its donated funds on the debt.

When a lender cannot collect a debt, the lender then sells that debt to a collector. Usually the lender sells the debt for a greatly discounted price. The collector who buys the debt is then free to try to collect it. In this situation, Rolling Jubilee purchased the debt, but rather than try to collect on the debt, the project instead forgave it.

A group of former Everest College students united to boycott paying their debt after the school abruptly closed.

Overall, the Rolling Jubilee project has collected more than $700,000 in donations over the years. Before it took on student debt, the project paid off $15 million in emergency room bills.

CHAPTER EIGHT

IN THE
FUTURE

Apocalyptic predictions abound when people consider what will happen to tuition if it continues on its current trajectory. Since 1978, tuition has risen four times faster than inflation, at an average rate of 6 percent per year.[1] Estimates show if prices rise at 5 percent per year, by 2030, four-year public schools will charge more than $40,000 in tuition, fees, and room and board each year. According to the same data, four-year private schools will cost students approximately $90,000 for a single year.[2] If they continue to increase prices by 6 percent, public schools will average almost $50,000 and private colleges more than $110,000.[3]

Some worry that tuition could rise continuously, halting only when the wealthiest of students cannot—or will not—pay.

Others believe student loan debt is the next economic "bubble" that will burst. Backers of this theory point to similarities between the student debt crisis and the housing crisis that led to the Great Recession. They worry if too many students default on their loans, the United States will once more face an economic downturn.

THE STUDENT DEBT BUBBLE

People who worry the student loan crisis will follow the same path as the housing crisis point to similarities between the two. Most alarming to them is the rapid increase in student debt. Between 2007 and 2014, the amount of student loans doubled, growing by an average of 11 percent each year. At its peak, mortgage debt grew an average of 12 percent each year. However, critics of the student debt bubble theory point out that the similarities end there. Far fewer Americans hold student debt— approximately 40 million—than held mortgage debt during the housing crisis, around 98 million. Furthermore, the amount of student debt the average borrower bears, approximately $29,000, is also considerably less than the average mortgage borrower held in 2007, approximately $93,000.[4]

These forecasts of doom may not come true. But the surging prices are not sustainable. If they do continue rising, it is certain schools will start suffering. Some smaller private schools have already been casualties of the increasing prices. These institutions are heavily dependent on tuition from students for revenue. But as tuition prices surge across the board, students are starting to look more closely at public schools, a relatively cheaper option. Decreased enrollments, then, mean small schools lose that needed revenue from tuition. To increase tuition would likely send more potential students looking elsewhere, and if the schools offer lower tuition, they will be unable to meet their operating costs. Either way, the schools face debt and possibly closure. As a result, schools must decrease their class offerings or merge with other schools. Or they may shutter completely. Moody's Investor Service estimated college closures may triple, to 15 per year, in the coming years.

REVERSING THE TIDE

With no consensus on the cause of tuition increases, it can be difficult to pinpoint how best to curb the rise. Some call for institutions of higher education to implement cost-cutting measures. People argue that because colleges are intended to educate, schools should cut funding for things not directly related to teaching and learning. According to these people, over-the-top amenities, unnecessary administrators, and athletics programs that require subsidies from tuition should be cut or diminished. They also point to the elimination of tenure as a way to halt rising costs. By replacing it with multiyear contracts, professors could continue having job security while also being held accountable to remain efficient. Less expensive salaries for presidents are also targeted as a way to cut institution costs. However, not all believe that these measures will stem the tide of tuition prices. Instead, they turn to increased government funding and regulation as a key way to keep prices down.

Overall, most agree some kind of student-loan reform must take place to slow the rapidly ballooning student debt. Current financial aid and loans are offered based on the financial situation of students as they go into college. Rather, some argue, more emphasis should be placed on students' earning potential after school. They note that students who earn philosophy degrees will likely earn less income overall than business majors, but under the current system, they may be saddled with equal amounts of debt.

"IT'S HARD TO SEE IT CONTINUING THAT MUCH LONGER BECAUSE YOU'RE GETTING TO A POINT WHERE IT'S GETTING TOO DIFFICULT FOR FAMILIES TO AFFORD COLLEGE. STUDENTS CAN ACCESS LOANS. BUT FOR HOW LONG ARE THEY WILLING TO TAKE ON MORE AND MORE DEBT?"[5]

— ROBERT KELCHEN, PROFESSOR AT SETON HALL

Critics also target the complexity of the US financial-aid system. As the system stands, families are required to fill out complicated forms about income, and they never find out how much aid they qualify for until it is nearly time to make a college decision. This complexity can deter low-income students from completing the process. Reforming the FAFSA process would enable students to see early on how much aid they could expect and would likely increase higher-education accessibility.

MOVING AHEAD

Experts predict big changes ahead for higher education. Not only will these changes help control the cost of college; they will also make the delivery of instruction and knowledge more efficient. Already the seeds of some of these changes are in play.

The role of online classes in higher education has been growing since the early 2000s, especially since massive open online courses (MOOCs) blasted onto the scene in 2011. But many also expect hybrid classes—or classes that merge in-person and online instruction—to grow in popularity. Hybrid courses allow students to watch

Peter Struck of the University of Pennsylvania records a lecture for his massive open online course on Greek mythology.

traditional lectures online and then receive face-to-face instruction with a smaller group. Offering part of a class online decreases its overhead costs, which frees up time for professors and thereby allows schools to increase the number of students in a class without having to hire additional faculty. This enables a school to earn greater revenue from the class. Early studies show students in these hybrid classes are as successful in these classes as

MORE TO THE STORY

A HISTORY OF MOOCS

Massive open online courses, or MOOCs, are exactly what the name suggests. They are large online classes available for anyone to take, without having to pay or apply. MOOCs first came into being in 2008, with a class called "Connectivism and Connectivity Knowledge." Two instructors in Canada taught 25 paying students in a brick-and-mortar classroom, while 2,300 nonpaying students participated online from around the world. Three years later, 160,000 students signed up for a single MOOC, "Introduction to Artificial Intelligence," offered through Stanford University.[6]

Since then, MOOCs have taken off. Highly regarded schools, such as Stanford, Harvard, and the Massachusetts Institute of Technology, have developed their own digital platforms. These allow the schools to disseminate online classes to an unlimited number of people remotely. And people from all areas of the world are eager for the opportunity to learn from some of the most elite researchers and professors in their respective fields.

The classes do not provide academic credit, although students who pass the courses can pay to receive a certificate of completion. In 2013, the American Council on Education reviewed some of the MOOCs on the market. The organization highlighted five courses and suggested schools offer their students credit for taking them.

in face-to-face-only classes, and the students require only three-fourths of the time to learn the material.

As the Great Recession drew to a close, analysts found more students were enrolling in community college. Those students were increasingly from affluent families. In 2015, approximately 25 percent of students from families with an annual income of more than $100,000 went to community colleges. This was 12 percent more than five years earlier.[7] If prices continue climbing, more people may complete their first two years of higher education at a community college, especially if President Obama's America's College Promise takes root. Also, some community colleges are upping their offerings to include four-year bachelor's degrees and pipelines to local universities.

THE CHANGING REPUTATION OF COMMUNITY COLLEGE

Astronaut Eileen Collins and journalist Jim Lehrer are two of the many famous graduates of community college. However, despite some individuals' success, community college has long suffered a bad reputation. For years, many people saw community college as a last resort for students unable to get in elsewhere. They thought degrees from two-year colleges were inferior to degrees earned at four-year institutions. These attitudes have been difficult to overcome, but recently they have been changing. Prestigious schools, such as those in the University of California system, are more actively seeking transfers from community colleges. They see community colleges provide valuable education for students, such as offering small first-year classes that some larger universities cannot provide.

IN THE FUTURE

A college degree will continue to be valuable in the future. Some experts estimate that by 2020, 65 percent of jobs will require applicants to have an associate's degree or higher, and approximately 35 percent of jobs will require a bachelor's degree.[8] But continuously surging tuition threatens the affordability of such degrees and people's access to them. High tuition is pushing these opportunities out of reach for more and more students.

To prevent this, numerous organizations such as the Million Student March are striving to reform the higher-education system. But until something changes, come each spring, students will wonder where they will go to college and also ask themselves how they will pay for it.

As high college debt remains an issue, students' concern over securing a post-graduation job becomes a larger pressure.

ESSENTIAL
FACTS

MAJOR EVENTS

- Since the early 1980s, tuition at postsecondary schools has tripled when accounting for inflation. Over the same period, median family income has largely stagnated, remaining at $64,000 per year. As a result, college tuition now eats into more of a family's earnings than it did in the 1980s.

- Explanations for the tuition rise point to tuition discounts offered to students, the natural rise in the cost of services, decreases in state funding, increases in federal funding, and overspending on amenities, administrators, and athletics.

- To combat this, three states have implemented programs for tuition-free community college. Similarly, President Obama proposed America's College Promise, which would offer tuition-free community college nationwide.

KEY PLAYERS

- Students and their families who must pay the prices spend years paying off debt, or they default on their loans.

- Schools that continue to raise their prices are trying to find ways to halt the trend.

- State governments that have cut funding to public higher education have also instated reforms to limit tuition increases.

- The federal government has increased funding and is seeking new ways to keep college affordable and accessible.

IMPACT ON SOCIETY

In 2015, student-loan debt surpassed $1.3 trillion, with more than 40 million borrowers. Students in the class of 2016 graduated with an average of $37,000 in debt. High student debt delays borrowers in reaching major life milestones, such as marriage, home buying, and having children. For some, the high tuition keeps them from attending college or causes them to drop out when they can no longer afford attending.

QUOTE

"Higher education can't be a luxury—it is an economic imperative that every family in America should be able to afford."

—President Barack Obama, State of the Union address, 2012

GLOSSARY

AFFLUENT
Well-off or wealthy.

AMENITY
A desirable feature that makes a place, such as a building, home, or school, more comfortable or valuable.

CROWD FUNDING
Raising money for a project by collecting small donations from a wide variety of people using the Internet.

DEFAULT
To fail to perform, pay, or make good.

ECONOMIC MOBILITY
The ability of a person to improve his or her financial status.

ENDOWMENT
A large amount of money that has been given to an institution, such as a school or hospital, and is used to pay for its creation and additional support.

INFLATION

An increase in the price of goods and services.

IVY LEAGUE

A group of eight elite, prestigious universities; the Ivy League includes Brown, Columbia, Cornell, Dartmouth, Harvard, Princeton, University of Pennsylvania, and Yale.

LAND GRANT

A gift of land by the government for colleges, roads, railroads, or other public projects.

NET PRICE

The tuition price that a student actually pays, after all scholarships, grants, and other subsidies have been deducted from the sticker price.

REVENUE

Income, especially of a company or organization and of a substantial nature.

SUBSIDY

Money paid, usually by a government, to keep the price of a product or service low.

UNDEREMPLOYED

Having less than full-time employment.

VOCATIONAL

Related to a trade, skill, or job.

ADDITIONAL
RESOURCES

SELECTED BIBLIOGRAPHY

Hacker, Andrew, and Claudia Dreifus. *Higher Education?: How Colleges Are Wasting Our Money and Failing Our Kids—and What We Can Do about It.* New York: Henry Holt, 2010. Print.

Schoen, John W. "Why Does a College Degree Cost So Much?" *CNBC.* CNBC, 16 June 2015. Web. 14 July 2016.

Selingo, Jeffrey J. *College (Un)bound: The Future of Higher Education and What It Means for Students.* New York: Houghton, 2013. Print.

FURTHER READINGS

Bryfonski, Dedria, ed. *College Admissions.* Farmington Hills, MI: Greenhaven, 2015. Print.

Bryfonski, Dedria, ed. *Student Loans.* Farmington Hills, MI: Greenhaven, 2016. Print.

Thelin, John R. *The Rising Costs of Higher Education: A Reference Handbook.* Santa Barbara, CA: ABC-CLIO, 2013. Print.

WEBSITES

To learn more about Special Reports, visit **booklinks.abdopublishing.com**. These links are routinely monitored and updated to provide the most current information available.

FOR MORE INFORMATION

For more information on this subject, contact or visit the following organizations:

American Council on Education
1 Dupont Circle NW
Washington, DC 20036
202-939-9300
http://www.acenet.edu/Pages/default.aspx
The American Council on Education is the leading organization devoted to higher education. Members come from all sectors of higher education, and the organization addresses all topics related to postsecondary education.

The Institute for College Access & Success (TICAS)
110 Maryland Avenue NE, Suite 112
Washington, DC 20002
202-223-6060
http://ticas.org
TICAS strives to make college more affordable and accessible for all Americans. It sponsors nonpartisan research and analysis and uses this to work to change public policy.

SOURCE
NOTES

CHAPTER 1. SURGING TUITION

1. Million Student March. "West Virginia University Photo." *Facebook*. Facebook, 12 Nov. 2015. Web. 28 Apr. 2016.

2. USA TODAY College staff. "Million Student March Protests Student Debt, Tuition Rates." *USA Today College*. USA Today, 12 Nov. 2015. Web. 5 Aug. 2016.

3. "What Is #MillionStudentMarch?" *Million Student March*. Million Student March, n.d. Web. 5 Aug. 2016.

4. Danielle Douglas-Gabriel. "Million Student March Fights for Debt-Free College." *The Washington Post*. Washington Post, 12 Nov. 2015. Web. 5 Aug. 2016.

5. "Average Published Undergraduate Charges by Sector, 2015-16." *CollegeBoard*. The College Board, 2016. Web. 5 Aug. 2016.

6. Danielle Douglas-Gabriel. "Million Student March Fights for Debt-Free College." *The Washington Post*. Washington Post, 12 Nov. 2015. Web. 5 Aug. 2016.

7. "Average Net Price over Time for Full-Time Students, by Sector." *CollegeBoard*. The College Board, 2016. Web. 5 Aug. 2016.

8. "Remarks by the President in State of the Union Address." *The White House*. The White House, 24 Jan. 2012. Web. 8 Aug. 2016.

9. John A. Boehner and Howard P. McKeon. "The College Cost Crisis: A Congressional Analysis of College Costs and Implications for America's Higher Education System. *ERIC*. Institute of Education Sciences, 4 Sep. 2003. Web. 8 Aug. 2016.

10. Kelley Holland. "The High Economic and Social Costs of Student Loan Debt." *CNBC*. CNBC, 15 June 2015. Web. 8 Aug. 2016.

CHAPTER 2. HISTORY OF HIGHER EDUCATION

1. John Adams. "John Adams to Mathew Robinson Jr." *Founders Early Access*. The University of Virginia Press, 23 Mar. 1786." Web. 8 Aug. 2016.

2. "Remarks on Signing the Executive Order on Historically Black Colleges and Universities." *The American Presidency Project*. The American Presidency Project, 28 Apr. 1989. Web. 8 Aug. 2016.

3. John R. Thelin. "Why Did College Cost So Little? Affordability and Higher Education a Century Ago." *Society*, October 2015. *EBSCO*. Web. 18 Apr. 2016.

4. Claudia Goldin and Lawrence F. Katz. "Why the United States Led in Education: Lessons from Secondary School Expansion, 1910 to 1940." *Harvard.edu*. Harvard University, 4 Dec. 2012. Web. 8 Aug. 2016.

5. Thomas D. Snyder ed. *120 Years of American Education: A Statistical Portrait.* National Center for Education Statistics. Institute of Education Sciences, 19 Jan. 1993. Web. 8 Aug. 2016. 55, Table 19.

6. "The Recession of 2007–2009." *US Bureau of Labor Statistics.* US Department of Labor, Feb. 2012. Web. 8 Aug. 2016.

7. "Tuition and Fees and Room and Board over Time." *CollegeBoard.* The College Board, 2016. Web. 8 Aug. 2016.

8. "Table 303.40. Total Fall Enrollment in Degree-Granting Postsecondary Institutions, by Attendance Status, Sex, and Age: Selected Years, 1970 through 2024." *Digest of Education Statistics.* National Center for Education Statistics, May 2015. Web. 8 Aug. 2016.

CHAPTER 3. SCHOOL SPENDING

1. Michelle Goldberg. "This Is What Happens When You Slash Funding for Public Universities." *The Nation.* The Nation Company, 19 May 2015. Web. 8 Aug. 2016.

2. Jonathan D. Glater and Alan Finder. "In Tuition Game, Popularity Rises with Price." *The New York Times.* The New York Times, 12 Dec. 2006. Web. 8 Aug. 2016.

3. "2016 Cost of Recruiting an Undergraduate Report." *Ruffalo Noel Levitz.* Ruffalo Noel Levitz, LLC, 2016. Web. 8 Aug. 2016.

4. Douglas Belkin and Scott Thurm. "Deans List: Hiring Spree Fattens College Bureaucracy—And Tuition." *The Wall Street Journal.* Dow Jones & Company, Inc., 28 Dec. 2012. Web. 8 Aug. 2016.

5. Nick Anderson and Danielle Douglas-Gabriel. "Nation's Prominent Public Universities Are Shifting to Out-of-State Students." *The Washington Post.* The Washington Post, 30 Jan. 2016. Web. 8 Aug. 2016.

6. Michelle Goldberg. "This Is What Happens When You Slash Funding for Public Universities." *The Nation.* The Nation Company, 19 May 2015. Web. 8 Aug. 2016.

7. Andrew Hacker and Claudia Dreifus. *Higher Education?: How Colleges Are Wasting Our Money and Failing Our Kids—and What We Can Do about It.* New York: Henry Holt, 2010. Print. 30.

8. "Weekly Address: A New College Scorecard." *The White House.* The White House, 12 Sep. 2015. Web. 8 Aug. 2016.

9. Andrew Hacker and Claudia Dreifus. *Higher Education?: How Colleges Are Wasting Our Money and Failing Our Kids—and What We Can Do about It.* New York: Henry Holt, 2010. Print. 30.

10. John W. Schoen. "Why Does a College Degree Cost So Much?" *CNBC.* CNBC, 16 June 2015. Web. 14 July 2016.

CHAPTER 4. DISCOUNTS, TECHNOLOGY, AND FUNDING

1. Mark Kantrowitz. *Research Report: Causes of Faster-Than-Inflation Increases in College Tuition.* Pittsburgh: FinAid Page LLC, 2002. Web. 20 Apr. 2016.

2. NPR Staff. "When Money Trumps Need in College Admissions." *NPR.* National Public Radio, 24 Apr. 2014. Web. 8 Aug. 2016.

3. William J. Bennett. "Our Greedy Colleges." *The New York Times.* The New York Times, 18 Feb. 1987. Web. 8 Aug. 2016.

4. Ibid.

5. Robert B. Archibald and David H. Feldman. *The Anatomy of College Tuition.* American Council on Education. American Council on Education, 5 Apr. 2012. Web. 8 Aug. 2016. 10, Figure D.

6. "Total and Per-Student State Funding and Public Enrollment over Time." *College Board.* The College Board, 2016. Web. 8 Aug. 2016. Figure 16B.

7. Michelle Goldberg. "This Is What Happens When You Slash Funding for Public Universities." *The Nation.* The Nation Company, 19 May 2015. Web. 8 Aug. 2016. 23.

8. Andrew Martin, and Andrew W. Lehren. "A Generation Hobbled by the Soaring Cost of College." *The New York Times.* The New York Times, 12 May 2012. Web. 8 Aug. 2016.

9. Michelle Goldberg. "This Is What Happens When You Slash Funding for Public Universities." *The Nation.* The Nation Company, 19 May 2015. Web. 8 Aug. 2016. 23.

10. Melissa Korn. "For US Universities, the Rich Get Richer Faster." *The Wall Street Journal.* Dow Jones & Company, Inc., 16 Apr. 2015. Web. 8 Aug. 2016.

SOURCE NOTES
CONTINUED

CHAPTER 5. EFFECTS OF HIGH TUITION

1. Jennifer Liberto. "I Will Graduate with $100,000 in Loans." *CNN Money*. Cable News Network, 19 Jun. 2013. Web. 8 Aug. 2016.

2. Ryan D. Hahn and Derek Price. "Promise Lost: College-Qualified Students Who Don't Enroll in College." *ERIC*. Institute of Education Sciences, Nov. 2008. Web. 8 Aug. 2016. 11, Figure 2.

3. Andrew Martin, and Andrew W. Lehren. "A Generation Hobbled by the Soaring Cost of College." *The New York Times*. The New York Times, 12 May 2012. Web. 8 Aug. 2016.

4. Michelle Goldberg. "This Is What Happens When You Slash Funding for Public Universities." *The Nation*. The Nation Company, 19 May 2015. Web. 8 Aug. 2016. 25.

5. John A. Boehner and Howard P. McKeon. "The College Cost Crisis: A Congressional Analysis of College Costs and Implications for America's Higher Education System. *ERIC*. Institute of Education Sciences, 4 Sep. 2003. Web. 8 Aug. 2016.

6. Jeffrey J. Selingo. *College (Un)bound: The Future of Higher Education and What It Means for Students*. New York: Houghton, 2013. Print. 41.

7. "Institutional Retention and Graduation Rates for Undergraduate Students." *The Condition of Education 2015*. National Center for Education Statistics, 28 May 2015. National Center for Education Statistics. Web. 8 Aug. 2016.

8. Tara Siegel Bernard. "A Brighter Job Market, for Some." *The New York Times*. The New York Times, 8 Apr. 2016. Web. 8 Aug. 2016.

9. Josh Mitchell. "School-Loan Reckoning: 7 Million Are in Default." *The Wall Street Journal*. Dow Jones & Company, Inc., 21 Aug. 2015. Web. 8 Aug. 2016.

10. Susan Tompor. "College Student's Nightmare: Loan Debt and No Degree." *USA Today*. USA Today, 7 Jun. 2015. Web. 8 Aug. 2016.

11. Kelley Holland. "The High Economic and Social Costs of Student Loan Debt." *CNBC*. CNBC, 15 June 2015. Web. 14 July 2016.

12. Ibid.

CHAPTER 6. SCHOOL AND GOVERNMENT RESPONSES

1. Lauren Camera. "Colleges Slash Tuition to Eliminate Sticker Shock." *US News & World Report*. US News & World Report L.P., 17 Sep. 2015. Web. 8 Aug. 2016.

2. Fiscal Federalism Initiative. "Federal and State Funding of Higher Education." *The Pew Charitable Trusts*. The Pew Charitable Trusts, 11 Jun. 2015. Web. 8 Aug. 2016.

3. "Pell Grants: Total Expenditures, Maximum and Average Grant, and Number of Recipients over Time." *CollegeBoard*. The College Board, 2016. Web. 8 Aug. 2016.

4. Roger Fillion. "Tackling College Tuition: Lawmakers Seek Ways to Help Students and Families as the Costs of College Soars." *National Conference of State Legislatures*. National Conference of State Legislatures, 1 March 2016: Web. 8 Aug. 2016.

5. Carla Rivera. "Transfers Show Community Colleges' Rising Reputation." *Los Angeles Times*. Los Angeles Times, 21 Apr. 2014. Web. 8 Aug. 2016.

6. "Pell Grants." *ACCT*. ACCT, 2014. Web. 8 Aug. 2016.

7. Lyndsey Layton. "Democrats Propose Tuition-Free Public College, Vow to Lower Student Debt." *The Washington Post*. The Washington Post, 13 Oct. 2015. Web. 8 Aug. 2016.

CHAPTER 7. THE FOR-PROFIT PROBLEM

1. Gretchen Wright and Shannon Serrato. "Default Rate Declines, Yet 611,000 Defaulted on Federal Student Loans." *The Institute for College Access & Success*. TICAS, 30 Sep. 2015. Web. 13 May 2016.

2. *New York Times* Editorial Board. "When the College Degree Is Useless and the Debt Is Due." *The New York Times*. New York Times, 11 Mar. 2016. Web. 11 May 2016.

3. James Surowiecki. "The Rise and Fall of For-Profit Schools." *The New Yorker*. Condé Nast, 2 Nov. 2015. Web. 8 Aug. 2016.

4. "Project on Student Debt: State by State Data." *The Institute for College Access and Success*. TICAS, 2015. Web. 8 Aug. 2016.

5. Ali Wong. "The Downfall of For-Profit Colleges." *The Atlantic*. The Atlantic Monthly Group, 23 Feb. 2015. Web. 11 May 2016.

6. Gretchen Wright and Shannon Serrato. "Default Rate Declines, Yet 611,000 Defaulted on Federal Student Loans." *The Institute for College Access & Success*. TICAS, 30 Sep. 2015. Web. 13 May 2016.

7. Ali Wong. "The Downfall of For-Profit Colleges." *The Atlantic*. The Atlantic Monthly Group, 23 Feb. 2015. Web. 11 May 2016.

8. "Corinthian Debt Strike." *Debt Collective*. Shuttleworth Funded, 19 Feb. 2015. Web. 8 Aug. 2016.

9. "CFPB Sues For-Profit Corinthian Colleges for Predatory Lending Scheme." *CFPB*. Consumer Financial Protection Bureau, 16 Sep. 2014. Web. 8 Aug 2016.

10. "Rolling Jubilee Student Debt Buy." *Strike Debt!* Occupy Wall Street, 16 Sep. 2014. Web. 8 Aug. 2016.

CHAPTER 8. IN THE FUTURE

1. John W. Schoen. "Why Does a College Degree Cost So Much?" *CNBC*. CNBC, 16 June 2015. Web. 14 July 2016.

2. Mamta Badkar. "Here Are Some Horrific Projections for College Some Day." *Business Insider*. Business Insider, Inc., 30 May 2014. Web. 8 Aug. 2016.

3. Stephanie Landsman. "What College Tuition Will Look Like in 18 Years." *CNBC*. CNBC LLC, 25 May 2012. Web. 8 Aug. 2016.

4. Allie Bidwell. "No Student Loan Debt Bubble." *US News Digital Weekly* 8 Aug. 2014. *EBSCO*. Web. 8 Aug. 2016.

5. John W. Schoen. "Why Does a College Degree Cost So Much?" *CNBC*. CNBC, 16 June 2015. Web. 14 July 2016.

6. "A Brief History of MOOCs." *McGill University*. McGill University, 2016. Web. 8 Aug. 2016.

7. Jeffrey J. Selingo. "What's Wrong with Going to a Community College? How Two-Year Colleges Can Be Better Than Four-Year Universities." *The Washington Post*. The Washington Post, 29 Jun. 2015. Web. 8 Aug. 2016.

8. Anthony P. Carnevale, Nicole Smith, and Jeff Strohl. "Recovery: Job Growth and Education Requirements through 2020, Executive Summary." *Georgetown Public Policy Institute*. Georgetown University, Nov. 2014. Web. 8 Aug. 2016.

INDEX

ABOUT THE
AUTHOR

Emily Rose Oachs graduated as a member of Phi Beta Kappa from the University of Minnesota, with a degree in communication studies. She has authored more than 30 nonfiction books for children and young adults, on topics ranging from natural disasters and biomes to geography and history. She also edits K–12 educational materials and nonfiction books for children.